Alexander Graham
Bell

Struan Reid

Heinemann Library
Chicago, Illinois

Designed by AMR
Illustrated by Art Construction
Originated by Ambassador Litho
Printed in Hong Kong/China

05 04 03 02 01
10 9 8 7 6 5 4 3 2 1

Library of Congress Cataloging-in-Publication Data

Reid, Struan.
    Alexander Graham Bell / Struan Reid.
        p. cm. – (Groundbreakers.)
    Includes bibliographical references and index.
    Summary: A biography of the prolific inventor best known for his work with the deaf and his invention of the telephone.
    ISBN 1-57572-366-2 (library)
    1. Bell, Alexander Graham, 1847-1922—Juvenile literature. 2. Inventors—United States—Biography—Juvenile literature. [1. Bell, Alexander Graham, 1847-1922. 2. Inventors.] I. Title. II. Series.

TK6143.B4R45 2001
621.385'092—dc21
[B]   00-024355

Acknowledgments
The Publishers would like to thank the following for permission to reproduce photographs:
Mary Evans Picture Library, pp. 4, 7, 9, 12, 19, 26, 32, 38; Science Photo Library/Sheila Terry, p. 5; Science Museum/Science and Society Picture Library, pp. 6, 13, 23, 25; Parks Canada, Alexander Graham Bell National Historic Site, pp. 8, 10, 15, 17, 18, 20, 24, 27, 29, 30, 33, 39, 41; Hulton Deutsch Collection Limited, pp. 11, 16, 35, 37; Collections/Anthea Sieveking, p. 21; Science Photo Library, p.28; Mansell/Katz Collection, pp. 31, 40; Ann Ronan Picture Library, p. 36; Science Photo Library/Laguna Design, p. 42; Science Photo Library/Rosenfeld Images Ltd., p. 43.

Cover photograph reproduced with permission of the Mansell/Katz Collection.

Every effort has been made to contact copyright holders of any material reproduced in this book. Any omissions will be rectified in subsequent printings if notice is given to the Publisher.

Some words are shown in bold, **like this.** You can find out what they mean by looking in the glossary.

Contents

A Changing World

By age 48, when this engraving was made, Alexander Graham Bell had already achieved worldwide fame.

The life of Alexander Graham Bell spanned 75 years and covered an age of great invention, discovery, and change. This period saw the height of the **Industrial Revolution** in Europe. Huge new factories, powered by coal and steam, were producing all sorts of goods. Some of the greatest changes took place in the field of communications. In 1847—the year Bell was born in Edinburgh, Scotland—railroads and the electric **telegraph** were only just beginning to open up the world. By the time he died in 1922, people were flying in airplanes and sending radio messages around the world.

A touch of brilliance

Early in his life, Bell was inspired by his **deaf** mother to teach other deaf people to speak. While he was investigating the methods of human speech and hearing, he also discovered the principles of the telephone. Several people contributed to the development of the telephone, but it was Bell's brilliant imagination that made it possible.

Bell's invention of the telephone revolutionized communications, and it continues to affect our lives today in ways that would have been unimaginable in his time. The telephone is one of the most important inventions of all time. Without it, many of the things we now take for granted—the radio, television, fax machines, and the Internet—would not have been possible.

Many interests

The invention of the telephone in 1875 made Bell rich and famous while he was still only in his early thirties. But he did not stop there. The remaining 46 years of his life were packed with ideas and experiments. He invented a vacuum jacket—a forerunner of the **iron lung**—following the death of his own infant sons from breathing problems. He designed kites, airplanes, and a **hydrofoil** boat. He developed better ways to breed sheep and co-founded the **National Geographic Society.** When Bell died, he was working on a project to **distill** drinking water from sea water. His interests and genius touched many areas, but Bell's name is known all over the world mainly for his invention of the telephone.

In Bell's original telephone system, the speaker and the receiver were separate parts, but they were identical.

Alexander Bell was born in Edinburgh, Scotland, on March 3, 1847. His family always called him Aleck. He was the second son of Alexander Melville Bell, Professor of **Elocution** and the Art of Speech at Edinburgh University. Professor Bell helped people with problems such as **stammering** to talk clearly.

Growing up in Edinburgh

Professor Bell's three sons, Melville, Aleck, and Edward, were at first taught at home by their mother, Eliza Bell. She taught the three boys the usual school subjects, such as history and mathematics, but she also gave them drawing and music lessons. Aleck was an excellent pianist, and music was very important part to him. Eliza had been **deaf** since childhood and the boys learned to communicate with her by using sign language. This had a profound influence on young Aleck's interests, and later on his career.

*Eliza Grace Bell, Aleck's mother, had been deaf since childhood. Aleck was to spend much of his adult life developing and teaching deaf and **mute** people to communicate.*

ELIZA GRACE SYMONDS

Eliza Grace Symonds (1810–97) was born in England. She had three younger brothers. Her father was a surgeon in the Royal Navy and died in 1818, when Eliza was nine 9 years old. Although she had been deaf since childhood, she was very intelligent and widely-read. She was ten years older than Alexander Melville Bell, and when they first met she was working as a teacher of drawing and as a painter of **miniatures.** They were married on July 19, 1844.

Edinburgh, like most large cities of the time, was smoky and dirty, and Aleck's father was worried about his family's health. He bought a second house outside Edinburgh near the sea, so that the family could get out of the city and enjoy the fresh air. Aleck loved the time the family spent there and enjoyed going for walks along the beaches and studying the plants, birds, and animals. He also spent a lot of his time trying to invent things.

In 1858, at the age of 11, Aleck was sent away to study at the Royal Edinburgh High School. However, his time there was not a success. He disliked the strict discipline at the school. He chose to study Latin and Greek, but he wasn't very interested in the formal classes. After four years at the school, he left without earning his **diploma.**

A new name

When Aleck was 11 years old, a former student of his father's named Alexander Graham visited the family. Aleck liked the man's name and, as a show of independence from his father and because his brothers each had a middle name, he added the name Graham to his own. From then on, he was called Alexander Graham Bell.

Aleck's father, Alexander Melville Bell, was Professor of Elocution and the Art of Speech at Edinburgh University.

A Year in London

Aleck's father was worried about his son's poor performance at school, so he wrote to his own father in London. The senior Bell believed that his grandson needed the space to develop his own personality, away from the **domineering** characters of his father and brothers. He suggested that Aleck should come and stay with him in London. Aleck's father agreed, and in October of 1862 Aleck, then 15 years old, boarded the train south. He later wrote that this was "the turning point of my whole career."

Aleck's grandfather, Alexander Bell, was the first member of the Bell family to become interested in studying and teaching speech.

ALEXANDER BELL

Aleck's grandfather, also named Alexander Bell (1790–1865), had begun his working life as a shoemaker in Scotland. He later became an actor and teacher of **elocution** at the University of St. Andrews in Scotland. It was during this period that he became interested in speech difficulties, especially **stammering.** He moved south to London, where he opened a school of speech. His son—Aleck's father—and later Aleck himself, continued with this family profession.

An inspiring teacher

Aleck's grandfather was strict, and he insisted that his grandson dress neatly every day and study hard. Together they read through the plays of Shakespeare, and Aleck learned many of the speeches by heart. Aleck's grandfather was a speech expert and taught Aleck many of his special skills. Although he was strict, he inspired Aleck in a way that his father and teachers had been unable to do. Aleck respected his grandfather, and they got along well with each other.

The London that Aleck visited was a thriving industrial city. The Thames River was a busy commercial waterway, and the London skyline was dominated by church spires and the brick chimneys of houses and factories.

In Bell's words:

"We became companions and friends," he wrote years later. *"The year with my grandfather converted me from a boy somewhat prematurely into a man."*

(From the memoirs of Alexander Graham Bell)

In the early summer of 1863, Aleck's father traveled south to London. He was amazed to see how different his son was. Aleck had grown up in many ways, changing from a clumsy, untidy schoolboy into a well-dressed and self-confident young man.

Another reason for Aleck's father's trip to London was to meet an inventor named Charles Wheatstone. Wheatstone had invented the first effective electric **telegraph** and, in the 1820s, he had also produced a crude speaking machine. He gave Aleck and his father a demonstration of this old machine and lent them detailed diagrams of it.

PUBLIC SPEAKING

As Aleck was growing up, lessons in elocution were very popular. There was no television or radio, so many people attended public lectures on new scientific discoveries, inventions, and the exploration of the world. Because they had no microphones or loud-speakers in those days, it was important that the lecturers were able to speak clearly, without shouting.

By the age of 16 or 17, Aleck was a confident young man.

"I think you should implicitly [without question] surrender yourself to Papa's judgement in this matter."

(Aleck's mother Eliza, writing to him to try and settle an argument between him and his father)

After a year in London, Aleck returned to Edinburgh with his father. There, he and his brother Melville studied Wheatstone's designs for the talking machine and built an improved version. They used a tin tube, a wooden box, cotton, and rubber. By blowing through the tube they could make it say "Mama." This project taught Aleck much about how the human voice worked.

Breaking free

However, once Aleck was back with his family, his father began treating him like a little boy again. He felt stifled by his parents and became restless and depressed. He wanted to break free and even considered running away to sea. At the last minute, he changed his mind and decided instead to become a teacher. He applied and was hired as a student teacher at a boarding school called Weston House in Elgin, north of Edinburgh.

Aleck's father now realized that it was time for his two older sons to start their adult lives. Melville went to study at Edinburgh University and, in August of 1863, Aleck started his job as music and **elocution** teacher at Weston House. He was only 16 years old. Even though some of the students were older than their new teacher, the self-confidence Aleck had gained in London made him seem very responsible and much older than he really was.

At this time, Aleck was also studying the **acoustics** experiments of a German scientist named Hermann von Helmholtz. Helmholtz had managed to produce artificial vowel sounds with a machine, using tuning forks and electricity. Aleck believed that Helmholtz had actually sent the sounds by electricity through a wire, in the same way **telegraph** messages were sent, rather than just making the sounds himself. Although he turned out to be wrong, it started him thinking about the possibility of sending speech over distances along an electric wire.

Hermann von Helmholtz (1821–94) was one of the greatest German scientists of the 19th century. His work covered many subjects, including mathematics, physics, acoustics, and **optics.**

Aleck taught for a year at the school and then spent a year at Edinburgh University, where he studied Latin and Greek. He returned to Weston House in September of 1865 and, now 18 years old, was promoted to assistant **master.** He then spent a year teaching at Somerset College in Bath, England.

During his time as a teacher, Aleck continued his studies of **phonetics.** He would spend hours in his room experimenting with his voice, touching his throat and cheeks with his fingers while making different vowel sounds so that he could feel the vibrations. The results of his experiments sometimes conflicted with his father's ideas, but Aleck was beginning to make great advances of his own in the field of phonetics.

Discoveries Before Bell

Michael Faraday was a brilliant scientist and an excellent speaker who communicated his ideas to the public through his lectures.

Much of the technology that made the telephone possible had been in existence for many years before Aleck was even born. But with imagination and hard work, he gathered together the pieces of information and organized them into a completely new invention—the telephone.

Electricity and magnetism

An English scientist named Michael Faraday (1791–1867) had become very interested in the relationship between electricity and **magnetism.** People had known about magnetism for thousands of years, and many people believed that electricity and magnetism must be related in some way. In 1820, a Danish scientist named Hans Oersted (1777–1851) noticed that a wire with an electric current running through it acted like a magnet, making the needle move on a compass lying nearby.

Faraday then found that when he charged a coil of wire with electricity, an electric current also flowed in another, separate wire coil nearby. He believed that this second current must have been generated by the magnetic effect of the first one.

In 1823, the English scientist William Sturgeon (1783–1850) made the first **electromagnet.** By passing an electric current through a wire wrapped around an iron bar, he created a magnet that could lift 20 times its own weight.

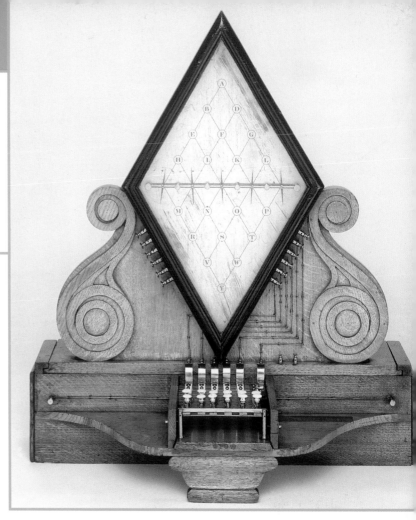

This needle telegraph was invented by William Cooke and Charles Wheatstone in England in 1837. Aleck and his father visited the two men in 1863 to learn about their inventions.

Messages along wires

The year 1837 was important in the development of the **telegraph.** In that year, Samuel Morse in the U.S. and England's William Cooke and Charles Wheatstone both **patented** effective telegraphs. Cooke and Wheatstone's machine had five needles that were induced by an electric current to point to letter on a grid. It was easy to read, but it required six wires to send the signal.

Samuel Morse's telegraph was based on the principle of **electromagnetism.** It sent electric pulses of different lengths that were recorded at the receiving end as dots and dashes. He developed a code—called Morse code—in which the dots and dashes represented letters and numbers.

Morse could not patent his telegraph in England because of Cooke and Wheatstone's claims. However, he successfully introduced his machine to the governments of other European nations, and it soon became the standard around the world.

In 1858, Charles Wheatstone devised an automatic telegraph system. Operators punched a message in Morse code onto a paper tape that ran through a transmitter. A pen at the other end drew the signal onto another paper tape. The pen was later replaced with a "sounder" to convert the dots and dashes into sounds that could be written down and translated by the operator.

Return to London

In April of 1865 Aleck's grandfather died. His son, Alexander Melville Bell, decided that the family work in **elocution** and **phonetics** should be continued in London. He, his wife, and their youngest son, Edward, traveled south and moved into Alexander Bell's old house.

Visible Speech

For many years, Aleck's father had been trying to invent a special alphabet to help people with speech difficulties, in which the signs would stand for sounds rather than letters. Using this alphabet, any sound in any language could be written down and read by someone else. After fifteen years of hard work, he finally produced his alphabet, which he called "Visible Speech." In the Visible Speech system, each symbol represented the positions of the mouth, tongue, lips, and throat used to make a particular sound. In this way, the sounds themselves could be written down.

Each of the 34 symbols in the Visible Speech system stands for a sound, not a letter. You can see that "six," "seven," and "saw" all begin with the same symbol, which represents the "s" sound.

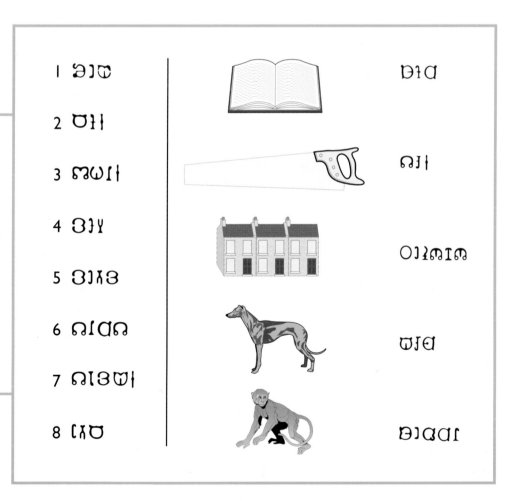

Aleck was very close to his brothers and his parents. His younger brother Edward, who died of tuberculosis in 1867, is on the right.

While Aleck was still teaching in Bath, tragedy struck the Bell family. Both of Aleck's brothers had suffered from bad health through much of their lives. In 1867 his younger brother Edward died of **tuberculosis.** The family was devastated, and Aleck hurried from Bath to London to be with them.

In 1868 Aleck **enrolled** as a student at London University to study **anatomy** and **physiology.** He worked hard at his studies and also helped his father to teach Visible Speech. At the same time he started a project of his own, teaching **deaf** children the basics of speech.

That same year, Aleck's father went on a lecture tour around the United States and Canada to demonstrate Visible Speech. No one in Britain had been very interested in the method, and he thought that it might receive more attention in North America. The trip was a great success, and Aleck's father began to think that the family's future might lie across the Atlantic Ocean.

He returned to London excited about the success of his American tour. Then tragedy struck the family a second time. In 1870 Aleck's remaining brother, Melville, suddenly became ill and died. The family, just recovering from their first loss, was shattered once again. Aleck's father decided that it was now time to leave for a new life in North America.

New Life in North America

Families board a ship bound for Canada in 1870. Like the Bells, they plan to start new lives in North America.

At first, Aleck wanted to stay in England. His studies at London University were going well. He also had a girlfriend named Marie Eccleston, and they were thinking about getting married. Aleck was at a turning point in his life—he had to decide which way to go.

An important decision

Aleck was now his parents' last surviving child, and he finally decided that it was his responsibility to accompany them to their new life in North America. After many sad farewells, the small family group sailed on July 21, 1870 from the port of Liverpool to Québec in Canada. Aleck was 23 years old, and a brand new chapter in his life was now beginning.

The Bells arrived in Québec on August 1, 1870. By the end of their first week in Canada, Aleck's father had bought a large white house in Tutela Heights, Ontario. It stood on 10 acres (4 hectares) of land and had an orchard with apple, plum, pear, and peach trees. The Bells moved in just in time to harvest the fruit!

The Bells' new house was not far from Niagara Falls, and the air was clean and fresh. Aleck spent the remaining weeks of the summer relaxing in the orchard, reading, and writing. It reminded him of his family vacations in the countryside outside Edinburgh. His health had suffered from the smoky London atmosphere, but by autumn he was feeling fit and rested and was ready to begin working.

Starting again

Aleck's father, meanwhile, was busy re-establishing contacts he had made on his lecture tour of Canada and the United States. He visited a number of cities, where he gave lectures on his Visible Speech system. While in Boston, he met Sarah Fuller, who ran a school for **deaf** children. She was very interested in Visible Speech and wanted it taught at her school. Aleck's father wrote home and mentioned this. Aleck immediately wrote back to his father to say that he would be very happy to teach at the school, even if he was not paid for it.

Aleck's father agreed, and Aleck was offered an appointment for one month at the Boston School for Deaf-**Mutes** (later called the Horace Mann School). He was to start work the next spring.

> **In Bell's words:**
>
> *"I shall not personally object to teaching Visible Speech in some well-known institution if you would get an appointment—even if it was not* **remunerative.***"*
>
> (Letter from Aleck to his father in 1870)

The Bells' house in Ontario was a pleasant change from busy London.

The Successful Teacher

On April 5, 1871, a fine spring day, Alexander Graham Bell stepped off the train in Boston and went to his new apartment. He was met by his **landlady,** who greeted him warmly. The next day he was given a tour of the city. Of all the buildings there, Bell was particularly impressed by the large public library on Boylston Street, and by the Boston Institute of Technology.

Sarah Fuller

Sarah Fuller (1836–1927) was a brilliant teacher of the **deaf.** She was born on a farm in Weston, Massachusetts and started teaching in 1855. Her career teaching deaf children began when she met the Reverend Dexter King, one of the founders of the Clarke School for the Deaf in Northampton, Massachusetts. She was later appointed principal of the school.

In 1869 the Boston School for Deaf-**Mutes** (later renamed the Horace Mann School for the Deaf) was founded. This was the first public day school for the deaf in the U.S. Sarah Fuller was appointed its first principal and worked there until 1910. The school was the first to adopt Visible Speech as an aid to teaching. Fuller and Bell kept in touch throughout their lives.

In Bell's words:

"I never saw Love, Goodness and Firmness so blended in one face before."

(Bell's description of Sarah Fuller just after he met her)

Alexander Graham Bell, in the top row at the right, began teaching at the Boston School for Deaf-Mutes in 1871. Sarah Fuller is second from the left in the fourth row.

Great impressions

The Visible Speech system made an immediate impact at Fuller's school. By the end of the first day, even the youngest students had made great progress.

Bell worked extremely hard over the following months at a number of schools. He was constantly improving and adjusting his teaching methods. But his skills were now so much in demand that he had to turn down offers of work in other parts of the country.

Boston, in the late 19th century, was an attractive and prosperous city.

Recipe for success

As the students' final exams approached, Bell became very nervous about the results. His work was still based on **trial and error,** and he was not sure whether his teaching methods had really been successful. But he shouldn't have worried. The superintendent of the Boston schools declared that the results were "more than satisfactory, they are wonderful!" He went on to say that Bell's teaching methods "must speedily revolutionize the teaching in all…deaf-mute schools." The Visible Speech system eventually became the standard method in North America for teaching the deaf to talk.

Bell spent the summer holidays with his parents in their home in Ontario. After a rewarding but exhausting time in Boston, he relaxed by going for long walks, riding, and swimming. Being back in beautiful, peaceful Tutela Heights allowed him to rest completely. It also gave him time to think, and while he was there he started to put together a long-term plan to open his own school for the deaf.

*Mabel Hubbard became deaf at the age of 5, as a result of **scarlet fever**. In 1872 Bell became her private tutor. Little did he know that she would turn out to be a special person in his life.*

THERESA DUDLEY

One of Bell's students was a 17-year-old girl named Theresa Dudley. Up until then, Bell had been teaching students whose deafness had been caused by illness or accident. But Theresa had been deaf from birth, so she had never heard a sound. Bell kept a detailed diary of his work with her, which recorded how, very slowly, he managed to get Theresa first to understand speech and eventually to speak herself.

While he was on vacation in Ontario, Bell had placed an advertisement in the newspapers, offering his services as a private **tutor.** But when he returned to Boston in September, he found that he had received only four responses. He began teaching this small group of students in his home. He was now 24 years old.

Patient guidance

Bell would demonstrate to his students how the sounds of human speech are produced by the very fast vibrations of the vocal cords in the **larynx.** He showed how the speed and sound of these vibrations could be changed by altering the position of the mouth, teeth and tongue.

Bell encouraged his students to touch his neck, jaw, cheeks, mouth, and lips. When he spoke, they could feel the vibrations. Then they would feel their own necks and mouths and try to make sounds that produced the same vibrations they had felt in him.

In Bell's words:

"I cannot describe to you the effect produced…I believe this experiment constitutes an epoch [important date] in the history of the education of the deaf and dumb [mute]."

(Letter from Bell to his parents, reporting his work with Theresa Dudley)

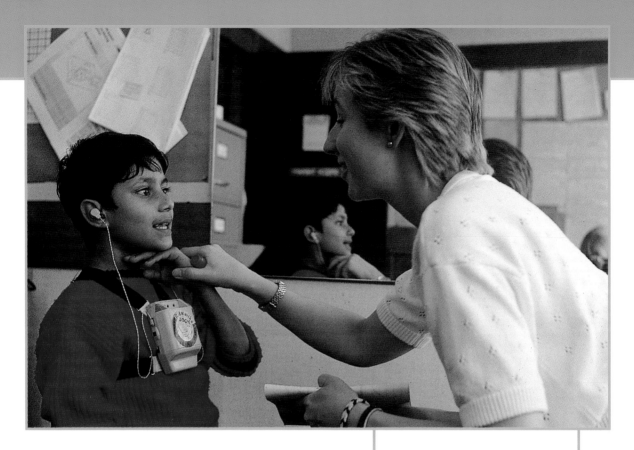

Bell tried to teach using patience and encouragement. This was quite different from the strict methods used in many other schools at the time. In this way, he built up his students' confidence and helped children who had been expected to remain **mute** their whole lives. He brought them great happiness, which he found very satisfying.

Bell continued to teach his small group of students. In March of 1872, he began teaching at the Clarke School for the **Deaf** in Northampton, Massachusetts, and at a school in Hartford, Connecticut. His teaching methods were once again a great success. He was in such demand that his classes were very large.

At the end of September, Bell returned to Boston and rented two rooms at 35 West Newton Street. It was his first permanent home in the United States. There, he gave private lessons to twelve students.

Deaf children today are still taught to speak by feeling the vibrations that speech creates in their vocal chords.

"With these simple motions...he has the whole two hundred and fifty voices, from deep bass to shrill treble, under sufficient control to make them roar in concert or die away softly...The pupils like it."

(A description of one of Bell's lessons at the Clarke School)

Improving the Telegraph

Bell had never forgotten the studies he made back in London and Edinburgh on Helmholtz's experiments on **acoustics.** During his time as a teacher, he spent many evenings in his rooms, trying to improve the design of the electric **telegraph.**

More than one message

One problem with the current telegraph was that it could send only one message at a time in each direction. This meant that lines were often busy and people had to wait to send messages. Bell's plan was to design a machine that could "read" several messages transmitted at the same time along the same wire. This would increase the number of messages the telegraph could handle, making it much quicker and cheaper to send them. He called his machine a "harmonic telegraph."

The harmonic telegraph

Bell's idea for a harmonic telegraph came from his knowledge of music and sound. If two string instruments, such as pianos or guitars, are placed next to each other and a note is played on one, the same note can be heard in the same string on the other instrument. This is called *resonance*, and the sound is carried from one instrument to the other by vibrations in the air.

Sound travels through the air as a series of vibrations called sound waves. When a string on a guitar is plucked, it produces sound waves at a particular frequency—or speed—depending on the note that is played. Another guitar nearby will be affected by these vibrations, and resonance will cause the same string on it to begin to vibrate.

Bell believed he could apply this principle of resonance to the telegraph, using vibrating electricity instead of air. He used a series of vibrating strips of metal attached to a wire to make an electric current switch on and off at the same rate as the vibrations in the metal strips.

At the other end of the wire, **electromagnets** were switched on and off by the electric current. Next to each electromagnet was another metal strip that would be attracted by the electromagnet. It would vibrate in resonance with the matching strip at the other end. In this way, each metal strip and its partner at the other end could send and receive their own message, without interfering with others being sent on the same wire.

Exhausting work

Bell's experiments on the telegraph took a lot of hard work. His idea for the harmonic telegraph may have been a simple one, but he did not have much experience working with electricity, and it took him a whole year to make his idea work.

After a year of teaching by day and working on the telegraph by night, Bell was worn out. He returned to his parents' house for Christmas in 1872. Rest and relaxation there brought him back to good health.

In Eliza Bell's words:

"We are grieved but not surprised at your being unwell. You undertake too much…We will talk of your invention …when you are home…I want you not to think about it just now."

On the Road to Success

In September of 1873, when he was only 26, Bell was appointed Professor of Vocal **Physiology** at Boston University. The university had opened just four years before. It was the first university in the United States to accept women as students.

Growing interest

As well as teaching at the university, Bell continued his work with his private students. This put him in touch with some very important figures in Boston society, who would have a great influence on his career. One of his students was Georgie Sanders, the 6-year-old son of a rich Boston businessman named Thomas Sanders. Another student was Mabel Hubbard, the 15-year-old daughter of Gardiner Hubbard, an important lawyer.

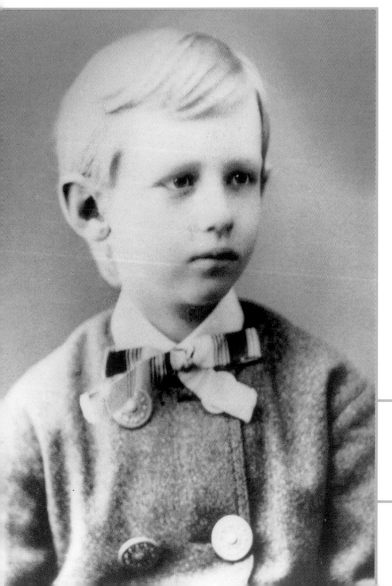

Meanwhile, whenever he had any free time, Bell continued with his experiments on the **telegraph.** He was eager for fame and fortune, and he knew that if he managed to design a multiple telegraph that could transmit a number of messages at the same time, he would become very rich. But his progress was slowed down by his lack of electrical knowledge.

Bell often went to an electrical shop in Boston, owned by a man named Charles Williams, to buy pieces of equipment for his experiments. One of the

Georgie Sanders had been born **deaf.** *After just a year of lessons with Bell, he was able to read and spell.*

assistants working in Williams's shop was a young man named Thomas Watson. Watson was a brilliant electrician, and soon he was helping Bell with his experiments.

Thomas Sanders and Gardiner Hubbard were very interested in Bell's experiments with the telegraph, and they agreed to become his financial backers. With their help, Bell was now able to afford to pay for an assistant. He chose Thomas Watson for the job.

Bell needed all the help he could get, because other inventors were also working hard on improving the telegraph. One of these was Elisha Gray of Chicago, and Bell wrote that it was "a neck-and-neck race between Mr. Gray and myself who shall complete an apparatus [machine] first." Bell and Gray had heard of each other's work through mutual contacts. The heat was on—and only time would tell who would reach the goal first.

Thomas Watson's skills as an electrical engineer were crucial in Bell's work on the telegraph and later on the telephone.

THOMAS WATSON

Thomas Watson (1854–1934) was born in Salem, Massachusetts. His father was the head of a local stable. Thomas started working at Charles Williams's shop when he was 18 years old, and within two years he was one of the best workmen in the shop. He worked with Bell for more than five years and became one of the founders of the Bell Telephone Company. He later took up farming and eventually became a successful shipbuilder.

A Change of Direction

The race to design an improved **telegraph** was fierce, and Bell and Watson worked hard over the following months. Sometimes Bell worked through the night until dawn. Finally, on February 25, 1875, he **patented** a device he called an "autograph telegraph." This used the multiple telegraph system to make dots and dashes on a strip of paper. It was a primitive version of the modern facsimile (fax) machine.

Joseph Henry was a pioneer in many scientific fields. He advanced our knowledge of electricity, radio waves, **magnetism,** and weather.

In March of the same year, Bell traveled to Washington, D.C. to meet the famous scientist Joseph Henry, director of the **Smithsonian Institution.** Bell gave him a demonstration of all he had achieved so far in his telegraph experiments. He also asked Henry for his opinion on an idea he had for transmitting the human voice, using a telegraph with a **diaphragm** instead of metal strips. Henry was very interested and replied that Bell had "the germ of a great invention." But when Bell said that he did not have the electrical knowledge needed to continue with this work, Henry told him, "Get it!"

In Bell's words:

"I cannot tell you how much these two words have encouraged me.'"

(Bell writing to his parents, soon after his meeting with Joseph Henry)

JOSEPH HENRY

Joseph Henry (1797–1878) was one of the most famous scientists in the U.S. He was born of Scottish parents and became professor of **Natural Philosophy** at Princeton University in 1832, and the first director of the Smithsonian Institution in 1846. As a young man, he had experimented with **electromagnetism** and designed the first electric telegraph. His encouragement played a vital part in Alexander Graham Bell's eventual success.

Gardiner Hubbard's financial support made it possible for Bell to continue his work on improving the telegraph, and then later on developing the telephone.

Henry's encouragement gave Bell the confidence he needed to develop his idea of the telephone. He decided to drop out of the telegraph race and to concentrate only on the telephone. But in order to devote as much time as possible to this new work, he quit working as a private **tutor.** The only students he kept were Georgie Sanders and Mabel Hubbard. This meant that he now had very little money to live on, and he was soon forced to borrow from Thomas Watson.

Gardiner Hubbard thought that Bell should continue with his work on the telegraph. He felt that it would be there that they would make their fortune. But Bell was growing more and more certain that he was on the verge of a breakthrough in the development of the telephone. Unknown to him, it would be only a matter of weeks before that happened.

In Bell's words:

"I think that the transmission of the human voice is much more nearly at hand than I had supposed."

(From a letter to his parents)

Accidental Discovery

On June 2, 1875, an extremely hot day in Boston, Alexander Graham Bell and Thomas Watson were working in the attic rooms of Charles Williams's shop, making adjustments to the multiple **telegraph.** They were in two separate rooms—Bell with three transmitters and three receivers in one room, connected by a wire to three receivers in the next-door room, where Watson was sitting. Batteries supplied electricity to the system. They were struggling to improve the design, and Bell was getting hot and impatient.

Falling into place

When he pressed the keys of the first two transmitters, the receivers in both rooms responded correctly. But when he tried the third transmitter, the metal strip on Watson's receiver did not respond. Bell thought that the strip must have become stuck, and he switched off the transmitters and batteries. As Watson plucked the strip to work it free, it vibrated up and down. Bell noticed that the corresponding receiving strip also started to vibrate, even though the electric current had been switched off.

Bursting with excitement, he ran next door and told Watson to continue plucking the metal strip and then ran back to his own room. To his delight, the strip continued to vibrate. As Watson continued plucking his strip, the metal strip on Bell's receiver not only continued to vibrate but also made a sound.

Bell's laboratory above Charles Williams's shop was often cluttered with electrical devices.

Bell suddenly realized what was happening. As Watson's metal strip vibrated up and down when he plucked it, it produced an electric current in the wire all by itself. This principle is known as *electromagnetic induction* and is the basis of the telephone. As the strip vibrated, the electric current in the wire changed in strength, which made the receiver strip at Bell's end vibrate in the same way. In that moment, on that hot evening at the beginning of June 1875, the telephone was born.

Electromagnetic induction

If a magnet or a piece of magnetized metal is placed near a wire, an electric current will be induced, or generated, in the wire. The **magnetic field** must move or vary in strength in relation to the wire in order for the electricity to flow continuously.

Two years before his accidental discovery, in 1873, Bell had come up with the idea of using a thin, magnetized metal strip vibrating at a set speed next to a wire. He thought that an electric current would be induced in the wire at the same speed of vibration. But he thought it would be of no practical use, because the electric current it produced would be too weak. However, this turned out to be the basis of the telephone.

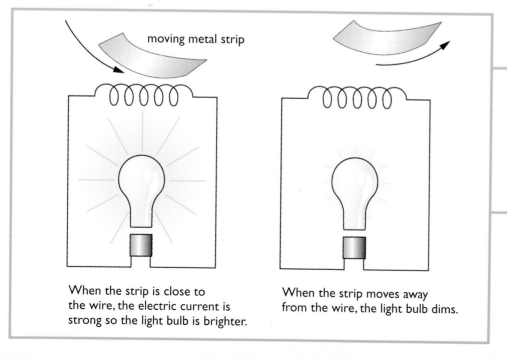

moving metal strip

When the strip is close to the wire, the electric current is strong so the light bulb is brighter.

When the strip moves away from the wire, the light bulb dims.

This diagram shows the principle of electromagnetic induction.

A Growing Love

Over the nex few days, Bell and Watson worked on perfecting the instrument. Bell felt that for the transmission of speech, a **diaphragm** would be better than a series of metal strips. He drew a rough design that he gave to Watson, who built a new machine in time for testing the next evening.

Trial and error

The device consisted of a wooden frame holding a sound receiver, with a metal strip touching a diaphragm made of **parchment.** But when they tested it, the diaphragm was too tight and thin and it broke. So they tried a thicker, stronger diaphragm, which—although it transmitted sounds when they spoke into it—did not allow them to make out any words. A lot more work needed to be done.

Mabel Hubbard had grown into a beautiful and confident young woman.

Bell was discouraged by these failures, and work on the telephone had to stop for eight months when Watson became ill—even though they were on the verge of a breakthrough. A number of other things were also developing, which now took up most of Bell's atention.

New concerns

Since March of 1875, Bell had been visiting the Hubbard home a few times each week to keep Gardiner Hubbard informed of the experimental work on the multiple **telegraph,** and also to continue his daughter Mabel's speech lessons. She was now 17 years old and Bell was 28. This was quite an age difference, but Bell realized that he was beginning to fall in love with his young student.

Bell had fallen out of favor with Gardiner Hubbard because he had abandoned work on the telegraph in favor of the telephone. Because of this, Hubbard was opposed at first to Bell's interest in his daughter. But, after some gentle persuasion, Mrs. Hubbard and Mabel eventually won him over, and on November 25, 1875, Thanksgiving Day—and Mabel's 18th birthday—she and Aleck became engaged.

The year of his engagement to Mabel Hubbard, Bell was on the verge of worldwide fame.

In Bell's words:

"I have discovered that my interest in my dear pupil…has ripened into a far deeper feeling…I have learned to love her."

(Part of a letter from Bell to Mabel's mother)

Who Was First?

Bell's life was about to change in all kinds of ways. In January of 1876 he rented two rooms at the top of a house in Exeter Place, Boston. He lived in one of the rooms and turned the other into a workshop. This was a critical time in his work on the telephone. He was still teaching during the day, and during the night he continued his experiments. He was on the verge of a breakthrough, but to protect his ideas he had to **patent** the telephone before anyone else did.

Unseen complications

Bell completed a detailed patent application in January of 1876. Because he was still a British citizen, he wanted to submit his telephone patent in England first. Everything was arranged, but the person he had entrusted to make the application in England decided at the last moment not to submit it—he felt that the telephone had no future.

At this point Mabel's father, Gardiner Hubbard, stepped in. Frustrated by all the delay, he acted on Bell's behalf and made a formal application for a United States patent in Washington, D.C. on February 14, 1876. He was just in time, because a few hours later a lawyer acting for Elisha Gray submitted a document claiming that Gray had invented a device for "transmitting conversations through an electric circuit." This document would have prevented others from trying to make a telephone.

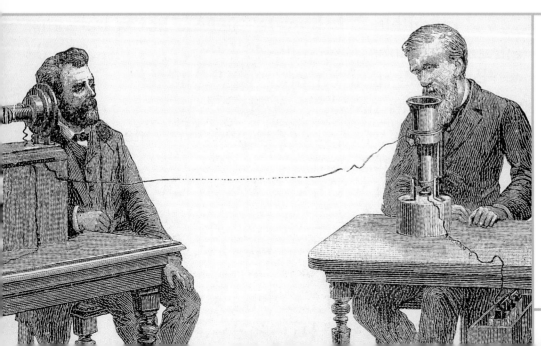

This engraving shows an imaginary telephone conversation between Bell (left) and Elisha Gray (right). Each man is using his own version of the telephone.

Gray had never tried out his device, so he had no proof that it worked. Bell was eventually awarded the patent for the telephone on March 7, 1876, four days after his 29th birthday. It would become one of the most valuable patents in history.

Elisha Gray admitted defeat at first, but later both he and other inventors tried to get the decision reversed. We know now that Gray's design would probably have worked better than Bell's. It was only a sketch, however—he had never built or tested his device. Hundreds of **lawsuits** were brought against Bell over the following years, but they all failed. In the race to make a telephone, Bell had won.

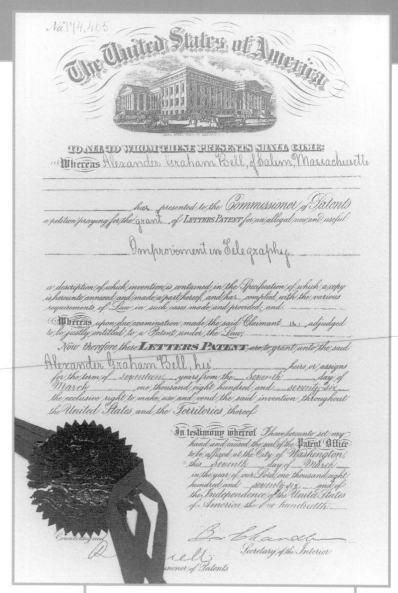

Bell's original patent—U.S. Patent number 174,465—for the telephone, dated March 7, 1876, gave him exclusive rights to the invention for 17 years.

The power of patents

A patent is a detailed description of an invention. This description is registered and held by the patent office to record the "first and true inventor." The person to whom the patent is issued is known as the *patentee*. For a set number of years, the patentee is granted the exclusive right to make, use, or sell the invention. The patentee can also grant this right to someone else, or they can sell the patent. If an invention becomes successful, as the telephone did, its patent is extremely valuable, because the person who has the patent for an invention also earns the money from the invention.

The First Telephone

On the day he was awarded the **patent** for the telephone, Alexander Graham Bell returned to Boston. Although he had won the race against Elisha Gray, there was still a lot more work to do on improving the telephone design before it would be useful. Bell made a drawing of another design and once again gave it to Thomas Watson to make.

Improved design

The new telephone equipment contained a **diaphragm** that vibrated when spoken into. A wire attached to the diaphragm vibrated with it. This vibration made the wire dip into a dish filled with a mixture of acid and water. Different sounds made the diaphragm and wire vibrate at different speeds, which in turn made the wire dip into the acid-water mixture at different levels. This variation changed the amount of electricity flowing through the wire. Finally, a receiver at the other end turned this electric current back into sound again.

This diagram shows how Bell's early telephone worked.

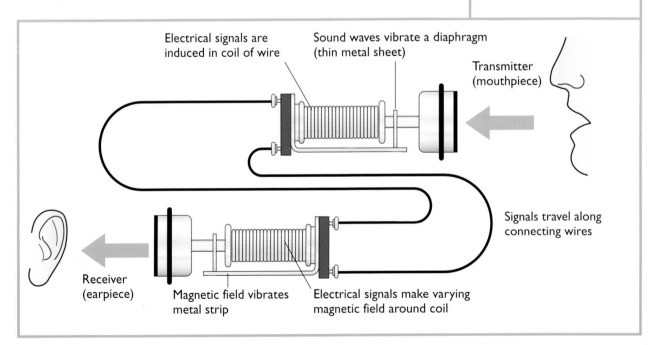

Electrical signals are induced in coil of wire

Sound waves vibrate a diaphragm (thin metal sheet)

Transmitter (mouthpiece)

Signals travel along connecting wires

Receiver (earpiece)

Magnetic field vibrates metal strip

Electrical signals make varying magnetic field around coil

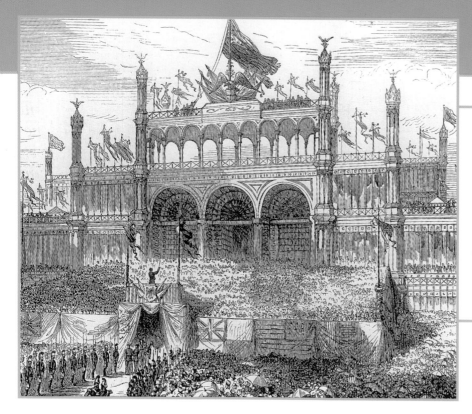

One of the most popular exhibits at the 1876 American Centennial Exhibition in Philadelphia was Alexander Graham Bell's amazing telephone.

The breakthrough had been made, but not everyone was convinced that the telephone had a practical use. Bell's challenge was to convince the public that it did. He needed a large public display in order to attract the support and money required to launch a telephone network that would challenge the power of the **telegraph** companies.

The opportunity arose when the 1876 **Centennial Exhibition** opened in Philadelphia. Many scientists and inventors from all over the world were going to be there—just the sort of audience Bell needed to show off his telephone. One important person visiting the exhibition was Pedro II, Emperor of Brazil. Bell gave him a demonstration of the telephone, and the event was such a success that it made the headlines in all the newspapers the next day. Interest was growing.

ELISHA GRAY

Elisha Gray (1835–1901) was born on a farm in Barnesville, Ohio. He became a boatbuilder, but also worked on improving the telegraph. In 1867 he patented a telegraphic relay switch. This invention won him the support of the powerful Western Union Telegraph Company.

He claimed to have thought of the idea for the telephone independently of Bell in November of 1875. However, he did not pursue his claim until the huge importance of Bell's invention became clear a few years later. Then the Western Union Company backed Gray's claim and contested Bell's patent for the next four years. Gray continued inventing in the field of electrical communication and became very rich, but he was always jealous of Bell's fame.

A Useful Device

News of the "miracle" invention was now spreading fast, helped by the many lectures and demonstrations that Bell gave all over the country. The world's first outdoor telephone line was installed on April 4, 1877 between Charles Williams's electrical shop and his house 3 miles (5 kilometers) away. In May, Bell and Watson held a telephone conversation between Boston and New York. The first business use of the telephone began in May, when a line was set up between the offices and home of a banker. The telephone was now on its way to dominating the world.

All change

On July 9, 1877 the Bell Telephone Company was founded, with Bell, Thomas Watson, Gardiner and Mabel Hubbard, and Thomas Sanders as the **shareholders.** Hubbard and Sanders took care of the important work of making and selling the new telephones. Two days later, on July 11, 1877, Aleck and Mabel were at last married, and Thomas Watson was their best man. Aleck was 30 years old and Mabel was 19.

Public demonstrations of the telephone, like this one in Salem, near Boson, were very popular.

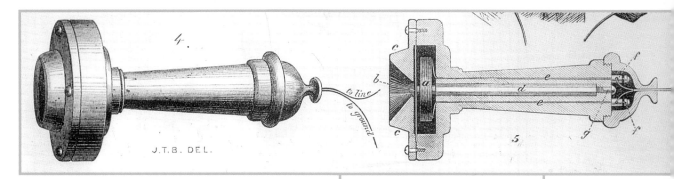

J.T.B. DEL.

After a brief visit to his parents in Canada, Bell and his new wife set sail from New York on August 4, 1877, bound for England. It was just seven years and three days since he had first set foot in North America, and in that time he had invented a device that was already beginning to change the world.

The transmitter-receiver telephone that Bell and Watson produced in 1877 was the first telephone on which it was possible to hold a two-way conversation.

Arriving in Plymouth, the couple traveled to London and Bath, then up to Scotland to visit Bell's childhood home in Edinburgh. In England, he gave a demonstration of the telephone to Queen Victoria, who later noted in her diary that it was "most extraordinary."

When Bell eventually returned to Boston, he worked for a while with the Bell Telephone Company. But he had no interest in being a businessman. He once wrote: "Financial dealings are distasteful to me and not at all in my line." He was also growing tired of the telephone, and irritated and upset by **lawsuits** from other inventors who claimed to have thought of the telephone first. In 1880 he resigned from the Bell Telephone Company but remained a shareholder.

In Bell's words:

"I went into his office that afternoon and found him talking to his wife by telephone. He seemed as delighted as could be."

(Letter from Bell to Mabel describing Charles Williams's telephone line)

Inventions and Married Life

Alexander Graham Bell was only 33 years old and already a very rich man. He could now devote his time to the thing that really interested him—inventing—and so he did, for the rest of his life. In the same year that he resigned from the Bell Telephone Company, Bell was awarded the prestigious Volta Prize for science by the government of France. He used the large amount of prize money (50,000 French francs) to set up the Volta Laboratory in Washington. There he worked on a device he called the "photophone," which he regarded as his greatest invention. This used a vibrating beam of light to transmit sound. The Volta Laboratory also worked on improvements to Thomas Edison's **phonograph.**

Air and sea

Bell worked on many other designs and inventions. He became especially interested in flying and designed many types of kites. One was a very light but strong design, known as a tetrahedral kite.

In 1908 Bell and his design team built an airplane called *June Bug* that went on to win the Scientific American flying trophy. They designed other successful airplanes, including the *Silver Dart*. Bell also designed a high-speed boat called a **hydrofoil,** which could skim over the surface of the water.

In a drawing made around 1903, Bell holds a model of his tetrahedral ("four-sided") kite.

The first successful hydrofoil had been built by Enrico Forlanini of Italy in 1900, but Bell's work improved the design. His HD-4 hydrofoil was 60 feet (18 meters) long and was powered by two 350-horsepower engines. In 1919 it reached a top speed of 71 miles (114 kilometers) per hour, a world record it held for ten years.

Bell became a respected leader in the world of science and invention, and the man who had never finished his college degree was now showered with honors from universities in the United States and Europe. He revived the ailing *Science* magazine and helped to make it the success it is today. As a co-founder and president of the **National Geographic Society,** he helped it become an international success.

Mabel and Aleck loved their two daughters, Elsie and Marian.

Mabel Bell

Mabel Bell (1857–1923), Aleck's wife, was one of three daughters of the Boston lawyer and businessman Gardiner Greene Hubbard. She was born on November 25, 1857 and lost her hearing when she was 5 years old as a result of **scarlet fever.** She and Aleck got married when she was 19, eleven years younger than him. They had two daughters: Elsie May, born on May 8, 1878; and Marian—called "Daisy"—born on February 15, 1880. Later they had two sons, Edward and Robert, but both died in infancy from breathing problems. Mabel had no more children and never got over the loss of the two boys. Elsie and Marian married and had a number of children of their own. Mabel gave $20,000 of her own money to set up the Aerial Experiment Association (AEA), the organization behind all of Aleck's flight experiments.

Final Years

Bell never forgot his work teaching **deaf** people to talk, and he continued to help people with hearing and speech difficulties. The money earned from some of his inventions went towards converting the Volta Laboratory into the Volta Bureau for the Promotion of the Teaching of Speech to the Deaf. He also continued his campaign to change the way people saw and treated those who had hearing difficulties.

Passion for inventing

Turning his attention to medicine, Bell designed a probe (a slender instrument) that could be used to find bullets hidden inside the human body. This made it possible for doctors to treat patients with gunshot wounds more successfully. It was used for many years, until it was replaced by X-ray photography. As a result of the deaths of his two infant sons from breathing problems, Bell designed a vacuum jacket. This was a forerunner of the **iron lung** and, when fitted around a patient, used air pressure to help them to breathe.

In 1886, Bell had bought some land on Cape Breton Island in Nova Scotia, Canada. Its wild beauty reminded him of his childhood vacations in Scotland. There, he and Mabel had a large summer home built that they named Beinn Bhreagh, which means "beautiful mountain" in the **Gaelic** language. For the next 35 years they spent every summer there with their daughters, and in time with their daughters' growing families. Bell also built a laboratory next to the house so that he could continue with his experiments even on vacation.

Bell opened the New York-to-Chicago telephone line in 1892.

> *"He is a magnificent figure of a man, and his dress—always the same—becomes him wonderfully. He wears long gray, coarse knit stockings with knickerbockers—or knee breeches—of grey tweed with a loose jacket plaited and belted."*
>
> (1911 description of Bell by Mabel's cousin, Mary Blatchford)

Summers at Beinn Breagh, the house on Cape Breton Island in Canada, were happy, restful times for Aleck and Mabel and their family.

In Mabel Bell's words:

"This morning we drove to the New Glen, and saw forest-covered hills, undulating valleys with trim, well-kept fields and neat little houses, pretty streams...I think we would be content to stay here many weeks just enjoying the lights and shades on all the hills and isles and lakes."

(Mabel Bell's description of Cape Breton Island)

It was at Beinn Bhreagh that Alexander Graham Bell died on August 2, 1922, with his beloved Mabel by his side. He was 75 years old and had been busy inventing right to the end. The funeral was held two days later, and when his coffin was lowered into his grave near the house, all the telephones throughout North America fell silent for one minute as a mark of respect to the father of the telephone. Mabel, brokenhearted, died five months later and was buried beside him at Beinn Breagh.

Alexander Graham Bell was a man with a burning curiosity about the world around him, and his passion for invention touched many different areas. But his name today is forever linked to the telephone. The Bell Telephone Company grew into American Telephone and **Telegraph** (AT&T), which is now one of the largest companies in the world. AT&T established the Bell Laboratories, where experiments could be made to develop improvements to the telephone and other forms of communication. It is now one of the world's most important centers of scientific research.

A shrinking world

The basic telephone that is used today is still based on the principles devised by Aleck Bell. But there have been many changes and improvements in dialing and switching systems since then. Bell had the idea of "talking with light" rather than using electricity to transmit sounds, and most of the main telephone networks today use light. The sound signals consist of patterns of laser light beamed along filaments of flexible glass called **optical fibers.** Each one is thinner than a human hair but can carry thousands of phone calls. **Digital** transmission now produces better sound and cheaper calls.

The radio was invented by Guglielmo Marconi 26 years after the telephone. The two technologies have been combined to create a communications revolution.

This late 20th-century mobile phone is also a video phone— the two people can see each other as well as speak to each other.

Today, most telephone systems transmit sound in the form of light, carried by optical fibers. Each fiber can carry thousands of telephone conversations.

Instead of wires, telephones can now use radio waves to transmit messages from one side of the world to the other, bouncing the signals off satellites far out in space. This has led to the dramatic increase, since the early 1990s, in the use of small, hand-held mobile phones that can be used almost anywhere.

Other kinds of information—not just sound signals—can now be converted into electrical or light signals and sent down a telephone line. In this way, letters, illustrations, and information stored on computers can be sent to facsimile (fax) machines on the other side of the world in a matter of seconds. Without the telephone, the Internet—which relies on phone connections— would have been impossible.

Legacy to the deaf

Bell's methods for teaching the **deaf** are still used in schools throughout the world. The Alexander Graham Bell Association for the Deaf, based in Washington, D.C., is now the largest organization for the education of deaf people.

The telephone has taken over our lives and transformed communications and human relationships in ways that would have been unimaginable in Bell's time. Thanks to his brilliant imagination and inventiveness, and his belief in the importance of communicating the human voice, the world has become a smaller place.

Timeline

1847	Alexander Bell born in Edinburgh, Scotland.
	The first commercial **telegraph** line in Edinburgh is opened.
1851	The first underwater telegraph cable is laid under the English Channel between Dover, England and Cap Gris Nez, France.
1855	James Clerk Maxwell devises a mathematical equation to explain the transmission of electromagnetic forces.
1858	Aleck **enrolls** at the Royal Edinburgh High School.
	He adopts the name Graham and becomes Alexander Graham Bell.
	First transatlantic cable laid between Ireland and Newfoundland.
	Charles Wheatstone **patents** an automatic telegraph system.
1861	A telegraph line is opened between New York and San Francisco.
1862	Aleck leaves school and stays with his grandfather in London for a year.
1863	Begins teaching in Elgin, Scotland.
1865	Father produces the Visible Speech alphabet.
1867	Brother Edward (Ted) dies of **tuberculosis.**
1870	Brother Melville (Melly) dies.
	Alexander Graham Bell sails to Canada with his parents.
1871	Begins teaching **deaf** children in Boston, Massachusetts.
1872	Starts experiments on the multiple telegraph.
1873	Appointed Professor of Vocal **Physiology** at Boston University.
1874	Makes his first sketch designs for a telephone.
	Gardiner Hubbard and Thomas Sanders become his financial backers.
	Thomas Watson becomes his assistant.
1875	Bell patents the "autograph telegraph."
	Accidental discovery of the basic principle of the telephone.
	Becomes engaged to Mabel Hubbard.
1876	Applies for and is granted a U.S. patent fot the telephone.
	Sends the first telephone message.
	Demonstrates telephone at the **Centennial Exhibition** in Philadelphia.
1877	Marries Mabel Hubbard and sails to England.
	Bell Telephone Company is founded.
	Thomas Edison invents the **phonograph.**
1878	Daughter Elsie born in London.
1879	Thomas Edison invents the electric light bulb.
1880	Bell resigns from the Bell Telephone Company.
	Second daughter, Marian, born.
	Awarded the Volta Prize for science.

1881	Bell and others invent a wax cylinder for Edison's phonograph. Emile Berliner patents a record player that uses flat discs. Son Edward born and dies.
1883	Son Robert born and dies. Nikola Tesla invents an induction motor.
1885	Heinrich Hertz begins research that demonstrates the existence of radio waves.
1886	Bell builds a summer home on Cape Breton Island, Canada.
1895	Wilhelm Röntgen discovers X-rays.
1898	Valdemar Poulson designs the forerunner of the modern tape recorder. Bell becomes president of the **National Geographic Society.**
1902	Guglielmo Marconi transmits the first radio message across the English Channel.
1908	Bell and colleagues win prize for the first manned flight of more than 0.6 mile (1 kilometer).
1911	Marie Curie receives the Nobel Prize for her work on radiation.
1915	Bell opens the first transcontinental telephone line between New York and San Francisco.
1919	Bell's **hydrofoil** boat breaks water-speed record.
1922	Alexander Graham Bell dies at Beinn Breagh, Cape Breton Island, Canada, aged 75. All the phones in North America fall silent for one minute to honor him.

More Books to Read

Fischer, Leonard Everett. *Alexander Graham Bell.* New York: Atheneum Books for Young Readers, 1999.

MacLeod, Elizabeth. *Alexander Graham Bell: An Inventive Life.* Buffalo, N.Y.:Kids Can Press, 1999.

Tames, Richard. *Alexander Graham Bell.* Danbury, Conn.: Franklin Watts, Inc., 1990.

Glossary

acoustics study of the properties of sound

anatomy structure of the body

Centennial Exhibition exhibition held to celebrate the 100th anniversary of the independence of the United States

diaphragm thin, flexible barrier

deaf unable to hear

digital transmitting information such as sound as a series of numbers rather than as waves

diploma document that states someone has earned a qualification or award

distill to purify a liquid through a process of evaporation and condensation

domineering exercising power over someone or something

electromagnet type of magnet produced by passing an electric current through a coil surrounding a soft metal core

electromagnetism magnetic forces produced by electricity

elocution art of speaking clearly and distinctly

enroll to sign up as a student at a school

Gaelic language spoken in Scotland and Ireland

heather plant with purplish-pink flowers that grows in hilly areas

hydrofoil motorboat with metal plates or fins attached that lift it out of the water when it is traveling fast enough

Industrial Revolution period of history when working practices and conditions were changed dramatically by the introduction of new machines and technology

iron lung rigid case fitted over a patient's body, in order to help him or her to breathe

landlady woman who rents rooms to people

lawsuit proceeding in a law court brought by one party against another

magnetic field region of magnetic force surrounding a magnet or an electrical source

magnetism power of attracting or repelling iron

master officer in the administration of a school or college

miniature small painted portrait, popular in the days before photography

mute unable to speak

National Geographic Society scientific and educational society established in 1888 in Washington, D.C.

natural philosophy physics

optical fibers thin glass fibers through which light can be sent

optics study of the properties of light

parchment type of paper sometimes made out of animal skin

patent government grant to an inventor, giving him or her the sole right to make, use, and sell their invention for a set period of time

phonetics sounds made by the human voice, and the study of these sounds

phonograph early type of record player

physiology way that the body works

remunerative offering payment, as a job

scarlet fever serious contagious disease that often involves a red rash and can leave survivors deaf or blind

shareholder person that owns a share of a business

Smithsonian Institution organization based in Washington, D.C. that provides funds for research and runs museums

stammering speech problem characterized by sudden stops and repetition of words or sounds

telegraph system for transmitting messages across distances using electricity

trial and error trying different solutions to a problem until one is successful

tuberculosis type of serious lung disease

tutor private teacher

Index

J	Reid, Struan.
B	
Bell	Alexander Graham
R	Bell.

$25.64   Grades 4-6

DATE			